Amedeo Clemente Modigliani

Pata Jo

The Master of Portrait Paintings Rediscovered faces 93

Rarete Art

"When I know your soul, I will paint your eyes."

Amedeo Clemente Modigliani

CONTENTS

Amedeo Clemente Modigliani, 1884-1920

Growing up in Livorno

Amedeo Modigliani was born in 1884 in Livorno, a town in the Tuscany region of Italy. Born into a prominent Jewish family, he grew up in the prosperous environment of a wealthy household during his early childhood. However, in his early teens, his family faced difficulties due to his father's business failure and a stroke. Despite facing health problems and various financial hardships, he developed a passion for art and eventually entered the world of art.

Artistic Features

Modigliani primarily created portraits and sculptures, characterized by their originality and simplified forms, influenced by Italian Renaissance, Mannerism painting, and African primitive sculpture. He uniquely expressed parts of the human body, such as emphasizing long necks and slender limbs, to depict the beauty of women. Additionally, he deeply considered beauty beyond traditional standards, developing a unique and modern concept of beauty. The forms and mature sensibilities of African art were reinterpreted through his works, offering a unique and contemporary perspective that inspired modern art.

Connections with Picasso and Brancusi

As a young man, Modigliani was active in Montparnasse and Montmartre, the artist hubs of Paris. At the time, the city was a gathering place for many renowned writers and artists, fostering diverse artistic exchanges. Modigliani expanded his artistic horizons by interacting with some of the greatest artists of the era, such as Pablo Ruiz Picasso and Constantin Brancusi. Additionally, the support of Paul Alexandre significantly aided his artistic endeavors. Alexandre, who lived in the same building as Modigliani, provided a foundation for his creative activities by facilitating meetings with various artists. It was also Alexandre who introduced Modigliani to the Romanian sculptor Brancusi. Under Brancusi's influence, Modigliani developed a painting style that expressed the inner spirit through simple and geometric forms. He also incorporated three-dimensional expressions and rich colors, influenced by Picasso's Cubism. In turn, Picasso drew inspiration from African art and archaeological forms in Modigliani's work, reflecting these influences in his own creations.

Portrait of Paul Alexandre(1909)

81 x 60 cm

Portrait of Paul Alexandre(1909)

100 x 81 cm

Tokyo Fuji Art Museum

Portrait of Paul Alexandre(1913)

80 x 45 cm

Musée des Beaux-Arts de Rouen

Portrait of Pablo Picasso(1915)

34.2 x 26.5 cm

Private Collection

Portrait of Picasso(1915)

Private Collection

Modigliani & African Art

In the early 20th century, African art brought a fresh breeze to Europe's art scene. Its simple, geometric forms and primitive expressions held a unique allure distinct from Western art, captivating many artists. Amedeo Modigliani was one such artist swept up in the African art craze. Around 1910, Modigliani encountered African art through Frank Haviland Burty. Burty was a collector and enthusiast of African art, and his studio showcased a variety of African artworks. Through these collected pieces, Modigliani became fascinated by the simplicity and geometric shapes of African art, as well as its primal expressions. He began incorporating elements of African art into his own work, evident in the elongated faces, long necks, and almond-shaped eyes seen in his portraits. Even the simplified, geometric forms in his sculptures bear the influence of African art.

Portrait of Frank Haviland Burty(1914)

73 x 60 cm

Los Angeles County Museum of Art

Portrait of Frank Haviland Burty(1914)

73 x 60 cm

Private Collection

Muse

A romantic and free-spirited soul, Modigliani fell in love with many women and captured their images in his works. His encounter with Beatrice Hastings occurred around 1914 in Paris. Hastings frequently appeared as a model in Modigliani's works. However, their relationship faced difficulties due to Modigliani's poor lifestyle habits, and they eventually parted ways after a short romantic period.

Modigliani enjoyed the repetitive task of drawing his models. Among these, he is known to have created over 25 works featuring Jeanne Hébuterne, his lover and fellow artist. Jeanne, a French woman, met Modigliani while working as a model at an art school. They fell in love at first sight and soon began living together. Jeanne was Modigliani's muse, inspiring him, while also being an independent female artist with her own artistic vision. They lived among the bohemian artists of Paris, receiving love and admiration from their peers. However, their love story ended in tragedy. Modigliani's life was marred by alcoholism, drug addiction, and poverty. Jeanne's parents disapproved of Modigliani and opposed their relationship. Despite this, Jeanne loved Modigliani deeply, cared for him devotedly during his addiction, and supported his artistic endeavors. After Modigliani died at the age of 35, Jeanne, stricken with grief, ended her own life at the young age of 21. Their love story is remembered as one of the most tragic yet beautiful romances in art history.

Beatrice Hastings Leaning on Her Elbow(1914)

Beatrice Hastings, 1914

Beatrice Hastings, 1915

35 x 26.5 cm

Beatrice Hastings, Seated, 1915

Portrait of Beatrice Hastings, 1915

81 x 54 cm

Portrait of Beatrice Hastings, 1915

Private Collection

Portrait of Beatrice Hastings, 1916

Private Collection

Portrait of Beatrice Hastings, 1916

Private Collection

Portrait of Beatrice Hastings in the hat, 1916

55 x 38.2 cm

Barnes Foundation, Philadelphia

Jeanne Hebuterne, 1917

129.5 x 81.6 cm

Private Collection

Jeanne Hebuterne with Hat and Necklace, 1917

164 x 137 cm

Private Collection

Jeanne Hebuterne with Necklace, 1917

55.5 x 38.5 cm

Private Collection

Jeanne Hebuterne, 1918

47 x 33 cm

Private Collection

Portrait of Jeann Hebuterne, 1918

92 x 60 cm

Portrait of Jeanne Hebutern, 1918

46 x 28 cm

Yale University Art Gallery

Portrait of Jeanne Hebuterne, 1918

46 x 29 cm

Private Collection

Portrait of Jeanne Hebuterne Seated, 1918

99.7 x 64.8 cm

Portrait of Jeanne Hebuterne Seated in a chair, 1918

92 x 60 cm

Private Collection

Portrait of Jeanne Hebuterne, 1918

Israel Museum

Portrait of Jeanne Hebuterne, 1918

100 x 65 cm

Private Collection

Jeanne Hebuterne with Yellow Sweater, 1918-19

100 x 64.7 cm

Jeanne Hebuterne, 1919

55 x 38 cm

Private Collection

Jeanne Hebuterne, 1919

91.4 x 73 cm

Metropolitan Museum of Art

Jeanne Hebuterne in a Scarf, 1919

88 x 56 cm

Jeanne Hebuterne in a Yellow Jumper, 1919

93 x 54.5 cm

Ohara Museum of Art, Kurashiki, Japan

Jeanne Hebuterne with White Collar, 1919

139.7 x 116.8 cm

Portrait of Jeanne Hebuterne, 1919

Private Collection

Portrait of Jeanne Hebuterne, 1919

55 x 39 cm

Private Collection

Portrait of Jeanne Hebuterne, 1919

91.4 x 73 cm

Portrait of Jeanne Hebuterne 1919

100.3 x 65.7 cm

Portrait of Jeanne Hebuterne with her Left Arm Behind her Head, 1919

Barnes Foundation, Philadelphia, PA, US

Portrait of Jeanne Hebuterne, 1919

55 x 38 cm

Jeanne Hebuterne in a Hat, c.1919

Private Collection

Chaïm Soutine

Modigliani and the Russian expressionist painter Chaïm Soutine had distinct artistic styles. Modigliani was renowned for his serene and sophisticated portraits, characterized by simple yet elegant lines and forms that expressed a tranquil and refined beauty. Soutine, on the other hand, pursued dynamic and intense expression through rich colors and unique brushwork, aiming to evoke emotions and power in his works.
These two artists, with their contrasting styles, interacted and influenced each other within the artistic community of Paris, particularly in Montparnasse and Montmartre. Their exchanges expanded their artistic perspectives, leading them to incorporate new ideas and techniques into their own works.

Henri Laurens

French sculptor Henri Laurens constructed a unique artistic world by creating sculptures that harmoniously combined geometric forms and human figures, reinterpreting traditional sculptural techniques with exceptional craftsmanship while reflecting the characteristics of industrialization and modern life.
Both Modigliani and Laurens shared a common interest in expressing human figures and emotions. Modigliani achieved this through painting, using simple yet elegant lines and forms to express serene and refined beauty. In contrast, Laurens expressed emotions alongside geometric forms in his sculptures. Over time, Modigliani increasingly utilized geometric forms to more effectively express human emotions and inner feelings.

Chaïm Soutine, c.1915

Portrait of Chaïm Soutine, 1916

100 x 65 cm

Private Collection

Chaïm Soutine, 1917

91.7 x 59.7 cm

Chester Dale Collection. National Gallery of Art, Washington, D.C

Portrait of Henri Laurens(1915)

Private Collection

Portrait of Henri Laurens(1915)

Private Collection

Max Jacob

Max Jacob was a French poet, writer, and painter who initially gained popularity as a poet and later engaged in various artistic endeavors, including art criticism. Jacob's literature was a significant source of inspiration for Modigliani. The abstraction and symbolism present in Jacob's works, the fusion of literature and art, his experimental techniques, and his emphasis on inner expression played a crucial role in helping Modigliani develop his unique artistic style and language. The interaction between these two artists deeply influenced each other, contributing to the advancement of modern art and taking it a step further.

Diego Rivera

Diego Rivera was a Mexican socialist painter and the founder of muralism. His works realistically depicted issues of the time, such as workers' lives, the gap between rich and poor, and social inequality, thus raising awareness in society. Influenced by Rivera's works, Modigliani began to reflect an interest in reality in his own creations. Conversely, Modigliani imparted poetic sensibility and experimental expression techniques to Rivera. While Rivera's murals were characterized by a realistic portrayal of societal issues, after meeting Modigliani, his murals began to exhibit a more poetic atmosphere and dynamic expression.

Portrait of Max Jacob, 1916

73 x 60 cm

Kunstsammlung Nordrhein-Westfalen, Düsseldorf, Germany

Max Jacob, c.1916

92.7 x 60.3 cm

Cincinnati Art Museum

Portrait of Diego Rivera, 1914

100 x 81 cm

Portrait of Diego Rivera, 1914

Portrait of Diego Rivera, 1916

100 x 79 cm

Museo de Arte de Sao Paulo (MASP), Sao Paulo, Brazil

Oscar Meistchaninoff

Oscar Miestchaninoff was a Russian sculptor with a keen interest in ancient Asian art. While working in Paris, he met and became friends with Modigliani. Modigliani painted portraits of Miestchaninoff, depicting his face almost as a caricature. The round face and awkward posture, along with clothing that somehow conveyed a childlike quality, were distinctive. Modigliani used a unique approach when drawing people, which he developed during his childhood in Livorno. His works often featured characteristic elements such as crooked noses and mouths, and very thinly drawn eyebrows. When depicting figures, he emphasized a childlike shortness of the neck, torso, and legs. The portraits of Miestchaninoff painted in this style are considered to express the pure emotions of Modigliani's childhood.

Moïse Kisling

Modigliani first met Moïse Kisling at the Académie Colarossi in 1913. Both being Jewish artists, they built a deep friendship through their shared background and their honest critiques and advice on each other's work. Kisling emphasized the importance of emotional and pure expression to Modigliani. They continued their artistic exchange by holding joint exhibitions and introducing each other's works. Despite financial difficulties, they encouraged each other with their shared passion for art, leading to mutual artistic growth.

Portrait of Oscar Meistchaninoff, 1916

Russian Sculpture Oscar Meistchaninoff, 1917

46 x 33 cm

Private Collection

37 x 28 cm

Palazzo Brera, Milan, Italy

Portrait of the Painter Moise Kisling, 1915-16

Musée d'Art Moderne de la Ville de Paris

Portrait of Moise Kisling, 1916

Lille Métropole Museum of Modern, Contemporary and Outsider Art (LaM), Lille, France

Paul Guillaume

Paul Guillaume was a French art dealer and one of the pioneers in introducing African art to Europe. He served as the dealer for Modigliani and Chaim Soutine while also engaging with some of the top artists of the time, such as Henri Matisse, Constantin Brâncusi, Pablo Picasso, and Giorgio De Chirico. By selling their works, Paul Guillaume played a significant role in the art market.

Léopold Zborowski

Leopold Zborowski, a Polish-born Jewish poet, writer, and art dealer, was also a key figure in the Paris art scene. He formed close friendships with many artists, including Modigliani, Chaim Soutine, Marc Chagall, and André Derain. Zborowski used his knowledge of the art market and sales strategies to bring attention to Modigliani's work. However, over time, conflicts began to arise as Zborowski attempted to limit Modigliani's artistic freedom. Modigliani, who highly valued his artistic vision and freedom of expression, often resisted Zborowski's commercial pressures. Ultimately, these conflicts made it difficult for their collaborative relationship to continue, and Modigliani had to pursue his artistic path independently.

100 x 75 cm

Musée de l'Orangerie

Portrait Of Paul Guillaume, 1916

81 x 54 cm

Museo del Novecento

Portrait Of Paul Guillaume, 1916

56 x 41 cm

Bellagio Gallery Of Fine Art, Las Vegas

Portrait of Leopold Zborowski, c.1916

116.2 x 73 cm

Leopold Zborowski, 1917

46 x 29 cm

Portrait of Leopold Zborowski, 1917

107 x 66 cm

São Paulo Museum of Art

Portrait of Leopold Zborowski, c.1917

Private Collection

Portrait of Leopold Zborowski with cane, 1918

73 x 50 cm

Private Collection

Portrait of Leopold Zborowski, 1918

46 x 27 cm

Private Collection

Portrait of Leopold Zborowski, 1919

The Beauty of the Marginalized

Modigliani did not hesitate to take as his subjects the marginalized sectors of society, such as impoverished artists, street people, and prostitutes. This was in stark contrast to the artistic trends of the time. In the Parisian art scene of the late 19th to early 20th centuries, the focus was typically on works for the affluent class, and dealing with the poor or socially marginalized was a deliberate artistic choice. Modigliani broke through these prejudices, choosing a unique artistic path by depicting the lives of the poor in his art. The marginalized figures in his works were portrayed with an emphasis on their human dignity and unique beauty. He did not view them as mere social outcasts but focused on their individuality and humanity.

He set up multiple canvases in his studio and worked on them alternately. This approach went beyond simple efficiency or practicality; it was about viewing the subjects from various perspectives and capturing their emotions. Modigliani aimed not just for realistic depiction but for expressing the essence and emotions of his subjects.

Modigliani suffered from tuberculosis since childhood and led a difficult life as an adult, struggling with alcoholism and drug addiction. Despite these hardships, his artistic achievements were remarkable. His distinctive mode of expression throughout his life transcended traditional standards of beauty, creating unique and innovative images. The profound expression of the soul and the intense emotions conveyed in his works significantly shaped modern art and continue to be greatly admired today.

The Cellist, 1909

130 x 81 cm

The Cellist, 1909

130 x 81 cm

Private Collection

Portrait of a Young Girl (Louise), 1915

51 x 37 cm

Private Collection

Almaisa, 1916

92 x 54 cm

Woman of Algiers (Almaisa), 1916

55 x 30 cm

Portrait of Dr. Devasena, 1917

Private Collection

Portrait of Dr. Devasena, 1917

55 x 46 cm

L'università di medicina di Johns Hopkins university, Baltimore

Chekhov Lunii, 1917

81 x 60.2 cm

Musee des Beaux-Arts, Grenoble, France

Portrait of Chekhov Lunii in white blouse, 1917

70 x 45 cm

Private Collection

Chekhov Lunii with her left hand on her cheek, 1918

55 x 47.5 cm

Private Collection

Portrait Of Chekhov Lunii, 1918

46 x 37.8 cm

Private Collection

Chekhov Lunii, 1919

80 x 52 cm

Museu de Arte Assis Chateaubriand (MAC), Campina Grande, Brazil

Portrait of Chekhov Lunii, 1919

46 x 33 cm

Private Collection

Woman with a Fan (Chekhov Lunii), 1919

Musée d'Art Moderne de la Ville de Paris

Hanka Zborowska seated in a divan, 1917

130.2 x 81.3 cm MOMA, NYC(The Museum of Modern Art, New York, USA)

Portrait of Hanka Zborowska, 1917

Portrait of Madame Zborowska, 1917

Zborowska, c.1917

Madame Zborowska, 1918

65.4 x 46 cm

Tate Modern, London

Hanka Zborowska, 1919

55 x 39 cm

Private Collection

Portrait of Zborowska, 1919

Private Collection

Elvira with white collar, 1918

92 x 65 cm

Private Collection

100 x 65 cm

Germaine Survage with Earrings, 1918

54 x 43 cm

Musee des Beaux-Arts - Nancy (France)

Portrait of Madame Survage, 1918

44.5 x 29 cm

Private Collection

Redhead Wearing a Pendant, 1918

Young Redhead in an Evening Dress, 1918

Self-Portrait, 1919

"There's not just one truth in the world, there are many perspectives."
- Amedeo Clemente Modigliani, 1884-1920 -